Procedures for Conducting Underwater Searches for Invasive Mussels (*Dreissena sp.*)

By Noah Adams

Prepared in cooperation with the U.S. Fish and Wildlife Service

Open-File Report 2010–1308

U.S. Department of the Interior
U.S. Geological Survey

U.S. Department of the Interior
KEN SALAZAR, Secretary

U.S. Geological Survey
Marcia K. McNutt, Director

U.S. Geological Survey, Reston, Virginia: 2010

For more information on the USGS—the Federal source for science about the Earth, its natural and living resources, natural hazards, and the environment, visit http://www.usgs.gov or call 1-888-ASK-USGS.

For an overview of USGS information products, including maps, imagery, and publications, visit *http://www.usgs.gov/pubprod*

To order this and other USGS information products, visit *http://store.usgs.gov*

Suggested citation:
Adams, Noah, 2010, Procedures for conducting underwater searches for invasive mussels (*Dreissena* sp.): U.S. Geological Survey Open-File Report 2010-1308, 44 p.

.

Contents

Figures

Tables

Conversion Factors

Inch/Pound to SI

Multiply	By	To obtain
	Length	
inch (in.)	2.54	centimeter (cm)
inch (in.)	25.4	millimeter (mm)
foot (ft)	0.31	meter (m)
mile (mi)	1.61	kilometer (km)
mile, nautical (nmi)	1.85	kilometer (km)

Temperature in degrees Fahrenheit (°F) may be converted to degrees Celsius (°C) as follows:
°C=(°F-32)/1.8.

Procedures for Conducting Underwater Searches for Invasive Mussels (*Dreissena sp.*)

By Noah Adams

Introduction

Zebra mussels (*Dreissena polymorpha)* were first detected in the Great Lakes in 1988. They were likely transported as larvae or young adults inside the ballast tanks of large ocean-going ships originating from Europe. Since their introduction, they have spread throughout the Eastern, Midwestern, and Southern United States. In 2007, Quagga mussels (*Dreissena rostriformis bugensis*) were found in the Western United States in Lake Mead, Nevada; part of the Lower Colorado River Basin. State and Federal managers are concerned that the mussels (hereafter referred to as dreissenid mussels or mussels) will continue to spread to the Columbia River Basin and have a major impact on the region's ecosystem, water delivery infrastructure, hydroelectric projects, and the economy.

The transport and use of recreational watercraft throughout the Western United States could easily result in spreading mussels to the Columbia River Basin. The number of recreational watercraft using Lake Mead can range from 350 to 3,500 a day (Bryan Moore, National Park Service, oral commun., June 21, 2008). Because recreational watercrafts are readily moved around and mussels may survive for a period of time when they are out of the water, there is a high potential to spread mussels from Lake Mead to other waterways in the Western United States. Efforts are being made to prevent the spread of mussels; however, there is great concern that these efforts will not be 100 percent successful.

When prevention efforts fail, early detection of mussels may provide an opportunity to implement rapid response management actions to minimize the impact. Control and eradication efforts are more likely to be successful if they are implemented when the density of mussels is low and the area of infestation is small. Once the population grows and becomes established, the mussels are extremely difficult, if not impossible, to control. Although chemicals may be used to kill the mussels, the chemicals that are currently available also can kill other aquatic life.

Early implementation of containment and eradication efforts requires getting reliable information to confirm the location of the infestation. One way to get this information is through the use of properly trained SCUBA divers. This document provides SCUBA divers with the necessary information to conduct underwater searchers for mussels. However, using SCUBA divers to search for mussels over a large geographic area is relatively expensive and inefficient. Early detection monitoring methods can be used to optimize the use of SCUBA divers.

Early detection monitoring can be accomplished by collecting water samples or deploying artificial settlement substrates (fig. 1). Water samples are used to look for free-swimming larval mussels (called veligers). Because the veligers cannot be identified with the naked eye, the water samples are sent to a laboratory where they are examined under a microscope and/or analyzed using molecular techniques to detect veligers. To detect the presences of adult mussels, artificial substrates are deployed and periodically retrieved to determine if mussels have settled on the substrate. If veligers or adults are identified, SCUBA divers can be deployed to confirm the presence of mussels.

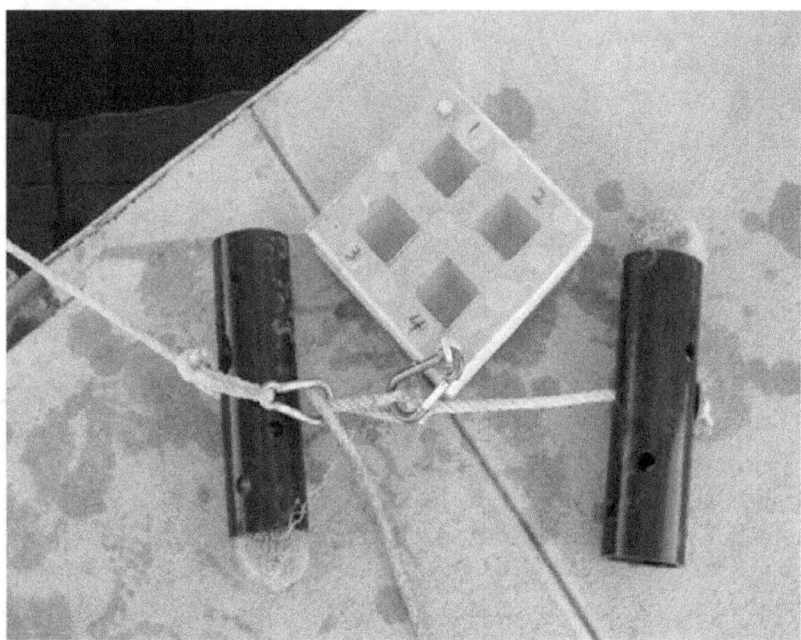

Figure 1.   Photograph of two types of artificial settlement substrate used to monitor for adult mussels. (Photograph courtesy of Bryan Moore, National Park Service, Lake Mead, Nevada.)

Background

The majority of divers that will be called on to conduct searches for mussels will likely have limited information on what they will be looking for. The following section provides basic information about mussels and a brief discussion on the importance of preventing the spread of invasive mussels.

How Mussels Move from Place to Place

Dreissenid mussels have two basic life history stages. The stage most people are familiar with is the settled adult stage. The other stage is the larval stage known as the veliger. The diagram in figure 2 shows the life cycle of the mussels. Adults produce eggs and sperm that are released into the water where fertilization occurs. The fertilized eggs develop into veligers that are subsequently transported by water currents. As the veligers develop and grow larger, they become less buoyant and sink to the bottom. Once on the bottom, the juvenile mussels attach to substrates (i.e., rocks, wood, and metal) and continue to grow into adults. As adults, they reproduce by releasing eggs and sperm into the water and the cycle is repeated. Once the adults settle, they can move around by detaching the thread-like material (called byssal threads; fig. 3) that holds them in place and float with the water current, or they can use their muscular foot to pull themselves along.

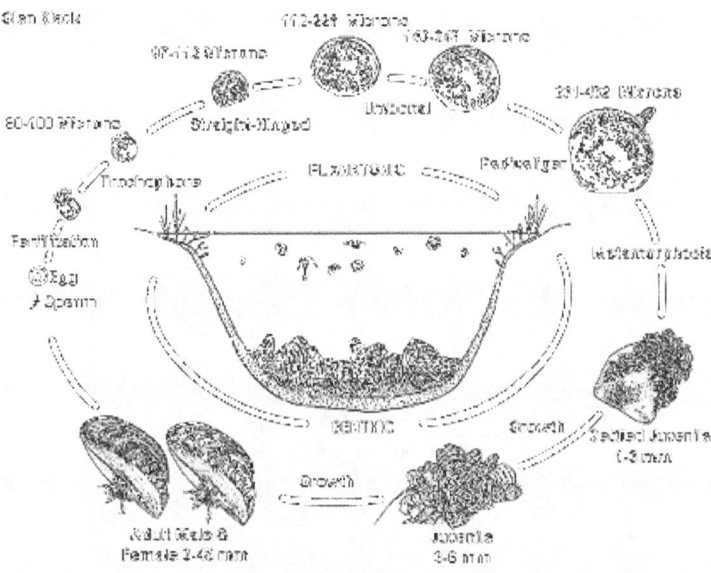

Figure 2. Diagram of the life cycle of dreissenid mussels.

Figure 3. Photograph showing a zebra mussel and the byssal threads they use to attach to substrates. (Photograph courtesy of Great Lakes Sea Grant Network, Exotic Species Library, Ohio Sea Grant project.)

The Importance of Preventing the Spread of Invasive Mussels

Impact on Aquatic Ecosystems

Mussels can have a significant impact on the aquatic ecosystem. A healthy ecological food web in lakes and reservoirs is highly dependent on the availability of microscopic organisms in the water. These organisms are the food for other larger organisms which in turn are food for even larger animals, like fish. When invasive mussels infest a lake, they filter the water and feed on the microscopic organisms, thereby depleting the availability of food for other organisms.

Impact on Native Mussels

In addition to consuming food that native animals depend on, mussels can attach themselves to other animals (figs. 4 and 5). This behavior, known as bio-fouling, can result in serious damage to native mussel and shellfish populations. When multiple mussels attach to the body of another animal, it can cause the animal to exert more effort to accomplish the normal activities necessary to survive. This increased effort can make it difficult to search for and capture food, more difficult to maintain their body temperature, and make the native animals more susceptible to parasites and disease.

Figure 4.   Photograph showing zebra mussels attached to a native clam. (Photograph courtesy of David Jude, Center for Great Lakes Aquatic Sciences.)

Figure 5.   Photograph showing zebra mussels attached to crayfish. (Photograph courtesy of GLSGN Exotic Species Library, Ontario Ministry of Natural Resources.)

Impact to Human Health

Because mussels are filter feeders, they can rapidly accumulate pollutants in their tissues. Some studies have shown that the level of toxins in mussels is 300,000 times greater than the concentrations of the toxins in the environment (Benson, 2010). These toxic chemicals can be passed to humans when they consume the meat of fish and waterfowl that feed on mussels.

Impact on Water-Related Structures

Mussels will attach to most hard surfaces and prefer locations where flowing water makes food and nutrients readily available. Water intake structures, like those used for power and municipal water treatment plants, provide an ideal environment for mussels (figs. 6 and 7). As the population grows, the mussels can clog the intakes and pipes and cause a significant reduction in pumping capabilities which could lead to a complete shutdown of the facility. The power industry has spent billions of dollars trying to eradicate mussel populations at hydroelectric facilities. The extensive infrastructure associated with hydropower and irrigated agriculture in the Columbia River Basin is particularly vulnerable to mussel infestations.

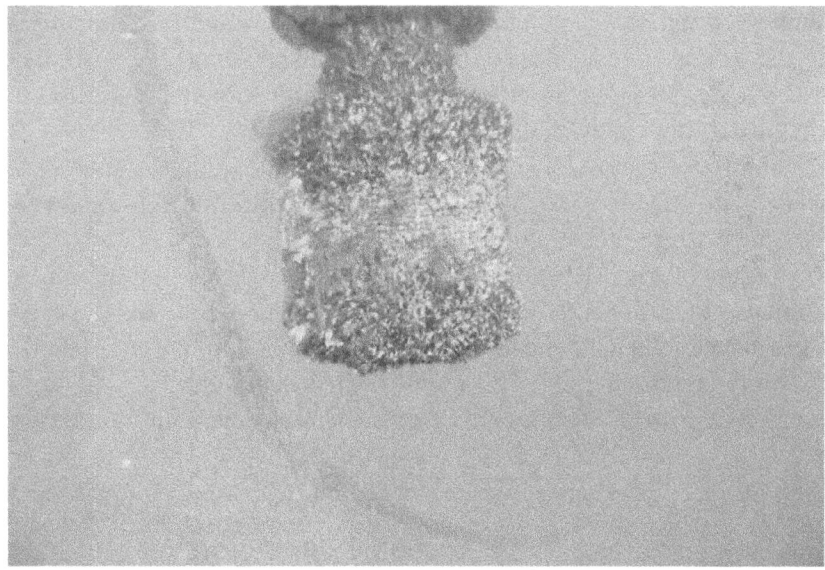

Figure 6.   Photograph of a water intake in Lake Mead, Nevada, with dreissenid mussel colony. (Photograph courtesy of Bryan Moore, National Park Service, Lake Mead, Nevada.)

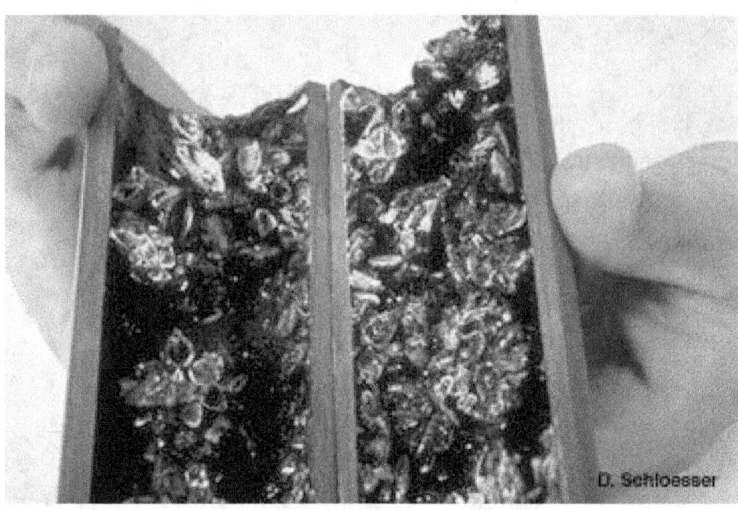

Figure 7. Photograph of a pipe that has been cut in half to show how the mussels can clog pipes. (Photograph courtesy of Don Schloesser, Great Lakes Science Center.)

Impact on Recreational Activities

Mussels can negatively affect the performance of recreational watercraft. When large numbers of mussels attach to the underside of a watercraft, the hull is no longer smooth. The increased roughness of the hull causes the engine to work harder to push the craft through the water (fig. 8). Attached mussels also can cause engines to overheat if they clog the cooling water inlets (fig. 9).

Swimmers, SCUBA divers, and people wading along the shoreline can be injured if mussels are attached to rocks, docks, and/or other structures. Mussels have shells with extremely sharp edges that can seriously injure unprotected skin and can cause damage to SCUBA equipment (figs. 10 and 11). In addition, SCUBA equipment must be decontaminated after diving in water that is infested with mussels to prevent spreading them to other locations. Chemical and hot water decontamination methods can damage SCUBA equipment. Lastly, mussel colonies can quickly obscure and degrade shipwrecks and the underwater landscape, thereby detracting from the allure of popular dive locations.

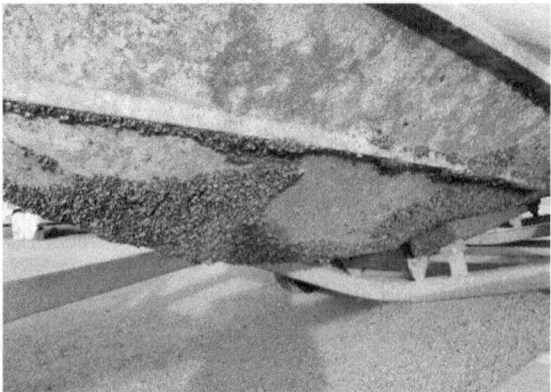

Figure 8. Photograph of mussel colony on hull of recreational boat from Lake Mead, Nevada. (Photograph courtesy of Bryan Moore, National Park Service, Lake Mead, Nevada.)

Figure 9.   Photograph of mussels on out-drive of recreational boat. (Photograph courtesy of Bryan Moore, National Park Service, Lake Mead, Nevada.)

Figure 10.   Photograph showing mussels on substrate in near-shore environment. (Photograph courtesy of the San Benito County Water District, California.)

Figure 11. Photograph showing mussels covering a beach in Great Lakes, Michigan. (Photograph courtesy of Stephen Stewart, Michigan Sea Grant project.)

Dive Practices

Good dive practices are critical to conducting safe and efficient searches for mussels. A rudimentary overview of good diving practices is presented below and is followed by detailed information about how to search for and collect mussels. Some of the methods and procedures presented are beyond the skill level of a newly certified, novice diver. It is the responsibility of the person overseeing the diving operations to determine if the divers are certified through a nationally recognized SCUBA-training organization and are capable of safely performing the activities necessary for conducting the searches.

Advanced Preparation

The request to conduct a search for mussels will likely be urgent and may only allow a day or two to prepare for activities at the dive site. Advanced training is recommended to prepare the divers to conduct the search in a timely, professional, and safe manner. A list of divers that complete advanced training should be maintained to simplify organizing and deploying a dive team when a request is made to conduct a search for mussels.

Divers asked to participate in a search will likely be members of various Federal, State, and local agencies. When divers from different agencies dive together, there are questions of liability that need to be addressed. One of the most important issues to consider is one of mutual competency. When a diver is put into a situation that is beyond their competency level, it can endanger all the divers on the mission. To prevent this from happening, the U.S. Geological Survey (USGS) requires divers from other agencies to meet minimum competency requirements before they can participate in multi-agency dive teams. Other Federal, State, and local agencies may have similar requirements.

Competency can be established in advance of diving operations by completing a reciprocity agreement. An example of a reciprocity agreement used by USGS is included in appendix 1. Establishing the reciprocity agreements between agencies is essential to allowing divers from different agencies to dive together and this information must be shared between agencies and reviewed and approved by the agencies Dive Safety Officers (DSO). Information that must be submitted for review includes dive logs, dive certification levels, number of dives in the last year, and results of last physical exam. In some cases, the DSO may request a diver to complete a "check-out competency dive" with the DSO or their designee.

Completing reciprocity agreements takes time, and should be done in advance of any potential request that requires divers from multiple agencies to work together. If reciprocity agreements are not in place before a search is conducted, divers from different agencies should not work together on the same team or dive in the same search area. Coordination between agency dive teams operating in the same geographic area can occur to prevent unnecessary duplication of effort.

Having agency divers working with non-agency diver is possible; however, there are some additional considerations that should be addressed. Typically, divers that are members of agency dive teams have met minimum standards that are above those needed for basic SCUBA certification. Additionally, most agency divers are covered under Workers' Compensation in the event of an injury. When non-agency divers are involved, it may not be clear who will cover medical expenses in the event of an accident. These issues must be addressed before non-agency divers are involved in searches for mussels with agency dive teams.

Dive Planning

Any time multiple divers are part of a search, it is necessary to identify roles and responsibilities (fig. 12). A Dive Operations Coordinator, often referred to as a Dive Master or Dive Team Leader, should be identified. In addition, an onsite Safety Officer should be identified. When personnel are limited, the Dive Operations Coordinator can also serve as the onsite Safety Officer. The roles and responsibilities of the Dive Operations Coordinator and onsite Safety Officer are shown below.

Figure 12. Photograph showing dive operations. Designated Dive Operations Coordinator shown on shore in colored hat, and/or a Safety Officer shown on shore helping divers with their gear. When multiple divers are used during a search, it is highly recommended that a Dive Operations Coordinator and/or an onsite Safety Officer assist the divers.

Dive Operations Coordinator

- Write a dive plan as required by the host agency.
- Coordinate pre-dive logistics to ensure that necessary equipment will be onsite (see appendix 2 for sample check lists).
- Establish reciprocity agreements and ensure documents are on file (see appendix 1 for example forms).
- Coordinate with the requesting agency's liaison to define the search area.
- Define search method and ensure that necessary equipment is onsite.
- Coordinate with divers to complete the search in a step-by-step fashion.
- Document environmental variables (see appendix 3 for sample data sheets).
- Document mussel samples collected by diver and transfer custody of samples to requesting agency (see appendix 3 for sample data sheets).
- Pre-seed the search area to assess effectiveness of the search (procedures for seeding a search area are discussed later in this document).
- Conduct pre-dive briefing including objectives, emergency procedures, and potential hazards.
- Conduct post-dive debriefing.
- Coordinate and document decontamination of dive equipment (see appendix 4 for decontamination protocol).

- Interact with the Press (Dive Operations Coordinator could be the primary person responsible for interacting with members of the Press. However, the agency responsible for the search may identify a person to serve as the public information officer. In this case, inquiries from members of the Press should be directed to that person.)

Onsite Safety Officer

- Assist divers with preparation of personal SCUBA equipment.
- Evaluate and monitor divers to determine if they are able to meet the requirements of the dive.
- Deploy and retrieve dive flags.
- Conduct pre- and post-dive checks with divers (see appendix 2 for sample check lists).
- Track entry and exit times of divers and monitor depths and tank pressures.
- Coordinate with surface support personnel to monitor the activities of multiple diver teams working in the search area.
- Interact with the public to keep the search area clear of unauthorized personnel. This could include keeping the surrounding area clear of unauthorized boaters.
- Work with the Dive Operations Coordinator to rotate dive teams into the search area in a timely and efficient manner.
- Assist Dive Operations Coordinator with decontamination of equipment.

Communication with Divers

Some search methods require communication between the divers and surface support personnel. Several of the search methods involve using a long rope attached to the diver and running back to a surface support person. The surface support person responsible for working with the diver at the other end of the rope is often referred to as the tender. The simplest way for divers and tenders to communicate is by pulling on the rope, often referred to as the tender line. Many different ways to communicate using line signals have been developed and no single way is necessarily better than another. A good communication system between tender and diver need only be easy to remember and easy to interpret. Table 1 outlines a simple way for the tender and diver to communicate using a tender line.

Table 1. A simple method for tender and diver to communicate.

Number of pulls on the line	Tender pulled the line to tell/ask diver:	Diver pulled the line to tell tender:
1 pull	Are you OK?	I am OK
2 pulls	You need to change direction	I am changing direction
3 pulls	You need to surface	I found something, stand by
4 pulls or more	Danger! Surface immediately!	I am in trouble! Send help!

Wireless communication equipment is another way for the tender and diver to talk to one another. Verbal communication between divers and surface personnel can increase the safety of the divers and eliminates the need to communicate using a tender line. The downside to using wireless technology is the cost to purchase the equipment to outfit the tender and diver ($3,000 to $5,000 dollars) and the additional training that might be needed to use the equipment.

The Buddy System

Regardless of the search method used, all methods should be conducted using the buddy system. The buddy system requires two divers to conduct the search while maintaining visual contact with one another. Each diver watches for anything that may impact the safety of the other diver. This can include helping each other monitor tank pressure to prevent running out of air and preventing each other from getting tangled in fishing line, ropes, or other debris. Some divers claim that the buddy system can present more dangers than diving solo. They argue that capable divers are often forced into dangerous situations by less-capable divers. However, most circumstances that can potentially endanger the divers are unexpected and often impossible to predict. Although an experienced diver can avoid more dangers than a less-capable diver, having a second diver during the search can provide assistance when something unexpected happens. In addition to implementing the buddy system, all search teams should have a backup diver (often referred to as a 90 percent diver) who has all their gear on and is ready to dive in a minutes' notice in the event of an emergency.

Identifying Mussels Underwater

What Divers Are Searching For

Searching for mussels will be new to most divers. Although many divers have experience searching for items underwater, few will have experience looking for something as small as mussels (fig. 13). There are two species of mussel the diver will be looking for: zebra mussel *(Dreissena polymorpha)* and Quagga mussel *(Dreissena rostriformis bugensis)*. They are collectively referred to as zebra mussels because of the characteristic zebra-like striped pattern on the shell (figs. 14 and 15). Because the striped pattern can be highly variable among individuals and difficult to identify in some cases, it should not be the only characteristic used to confirm the identity of the species.

When mussels are first introduced they often attach to the undersides of rocks (fig. 16), and in cracks and crevices of docks. As a result, divers must methodically examine all cracks and crevices to be confident they did a thorough job looking for mussels. To help increase the likelihood of finding mussels, divers should use a flashlight to examine dark crevices in rocks and other structures. If the search is being conducted in very turbid water and visibility is extremely low (that is, less than a couple of inches), divers can use a plastic bag filled with clear water to improve their ability to see the mussels. To use this method, the water-filled bag is placed over the top of the item that the diver is trying to identify. The diver then shines their flashlight through the side of the bag while pressing their dive mask against the bag. This allows the diver to view the object through the clear water inside the bag. After mussels become established and their population density increases, they are very easy to find. If mussels are found, the diver will need to collect a sample. Procedures for collecting and preserving samples are discussed later in this document.

Figure 13. Photograph showing the range of sizes of adult mussels. (Photograph courtesy of San Benito County Water District.)

Figure 14. Photograph of the two species of mussel commonly referred to as zebra mussels. The specimen in the top photograph is a zebra mussel and the specimen in the bottom of the photograph is a quagga mussel. (Photograph courtesy of U.S. Geological Survey.)

Figure 15. Photograph showing variation in the striped pattern of the shells of zebra mussels. (Photograph courtesy of U.S. Geological Survey.)

Figure 16. Photograph showing mussels attached to a rock. When mussels are first introduced in an area, it is common to find them tucked under the edge of rocks and in cracks and crevices of docks. (Photograph courtesy of Bryan Moore, Lake Mead National Park Service.)

What Divers Are Not Searching For

There are several native and non-native freshwater mussels and clams that could be present during a search for dreissenid mussels. One such species is the Asian clam (*Corbicula fluminea*). Asian clams are native to Southeast Asia and were first reported on the West Coast of the United States in the 1930s. Since then, Asian clams have spread to more than 39 States including the Pacific Northwest. It is relatively easy to tell the difference between Asian clams and dreissenid mussels. Some of the key differences between these two species are outlined in table 2 and displayed in figure 17. Nedeauand (2009) provides a more complete description of the freshwater mussels and clams that are present in the Pacific Northwest.

If a specimen is found during a search and the diver is not certain which species it is, the agency responsible for overseeing the search may request the diver to collect a sample so it can be identified by an expert. However, there are several species of mussels and clams that are protected under the Endangered Species Act (ESA) because their populations are threatened or endangered. Divers should not collect specimens unless the agency overseeing the search has the necessary authorization and permits.

Table 2.   Differences between Asian clams and dreissenid mussels.

Asian clam	Dreissenid Mussel
Generally larger than dreissenid mussels	Generally smaller than Asian clams
Found on the bottom in the mud	Found attached to structures
Light green/light brown colored shells	Dark stripes on a light colored shell
Distinctive ridges on shells	Smooth shells
Symmetrical shell	Shell skewed to one side

Figure 17.   Photograph showing differences between Asian clams and dreissenid mussels. The two specimens in the left of the photograph are Asian clams. The specimen to the left of the penny is a dreissenid mussel. The horizontal line under the specimen in the left of the photograph is 1 inch in length.

15

Defining the Search Area

Areas that are accessible without using divers should be searched before divers are deployed. If the purpose of the search is simply to confirm the presence of mussels, the shoreline and above water portions of docks can be searched for discarded shells. Rodents and birds that prey on mussels will use these areas to feed and often leave the shells behind. Similarly, a person in waders can easily search the shallow shoreline areas. If visibility is poor, rocks can be removed and inspected for attached mussels. Searching in shallow water and on docks and beaches for discarded shells can be done before the dive team is called to the site. Similarly, artificial settlement substrate, as discussed earlier, can be used to monitor an area for the presences of adult mussels before divers are deployed to search the area. However, artificial substrate monitoring is not 100 percent effective and should not be the only method used to monitor for the presence of adult mussels.

The feeding habits of the mussels can be used to prioritize which areas should be searched first. Because mussels are filter feeders (fig. 18), they require a constant supply of nutrient rich water to survive and reproduce. Water intake pipes offer an ideal habitat for mussels and should be searched first. However, severe injury or death can occur if a diver becomes impinged on an intake pipe. Therefore, searching intake pipes requires coordination with the operator of the intake to establish proper lock-out/tag-out procedures (appendix 5). Procedures must be in place to prevent the accidental operation of the intake while divers are in the area.

Figure 18. Photograph showing a colony of dreissenid mussels. The mussels filter the water for food and nutrients. Note that their shells are open and their tube-like siphon is extended to pull water into their digestive system. (Photograph courtesy of Marc Blouin, U.S. Geological Survey.)

Methods for Searching

The size of the search area, complexity of the structures that need to be searched, and the environmental characteristics of the search area are factors that determine which search method to use. The following section discusses some general considerations regardless of the specific search method and then outlines a few basic search methods that can be use under a variety of conditions.

General Considerations

If the search area is large and multiple divers will be used simultaneously, a Dive Operations Coordinator and an onsite Safety Officer should be designated. It is potentially dangerous to have multiple dive teams in the water simultaneously without having adequate surface support personnel to record the entry and exits of multiple dive teams and to ensure all safety procedures are being followed.

Safety of the divers is the primary concern when conducting searches. Divers need to keep safety at the forefront of their thoughts at all times. The more that is asked of a diver, the harder this is to accomplish. To limit what is asked of the divers, and to increase the probability of finding mussels, divers should only be asked to identify and collect invasive mussels during a search. If divers are asked to identify other species, like fish and other native clams or mussels, the probability of finding invasive mussels will decrease. Studies show that the more items a person is asked to include in the search, the lower the efficacy is for any single item (Henke, 1998). If there is interest in identifying other species within the search area, they should be searched for on subsequent dives, not the initial search for invasive mussels.

Regardless of the methods used to search for mussels, divers can increase the probability of finding mussels by keeping in mind that mussels need a substrate to attach to and they prefer settling in areas that have a continuous flow of nutrient rich water. With this in mind, divers can spend less time searching sandy or muddy areas and more time searching rocks and other structures.

Water current should always be considered when selecting and implementing a search method. When water velocity is less than 2 knots, a tender line can be used to guide the search and ensure that the divers are not inadvertently missing areas while they work against the current to maintain a search pattern. The search should progress into the current when possible so that sediment displaced by the divers is carried by the current into the area that has already been searched, not into the area that has yet to be searched. Conducting searches in water currents greater than 2 knots is not recommended unless the divers have had specific training and experience.

Arc Search Method

This method is good for searching shorelines or the area next to docks and boat ramps. Using this method, the diver searches along consecutive arcs that increase in size until the area of interest has been covered. A rope attached to the diver is used by a tender on shore to help guide the diver during the search. After completing an arc, the tender signals the diver to change directions. The tender lets out additional line and the diver changes direction, takes up the slack in the line, and proceeds on the next arc. At the end of the arc, the sequence is repeated and additional arcs are searched. The amount of line let out by the tender will determine the spacing between the arcs. The spacing between the arcs is in turn determined by the clarity of the water. In relatively clear water with visibility greater than 3 ft, a diver can adequately search an area 5 ft wide when looking for something as small as mussels. If each of the two divers in the buddy team can adequately search a 5-ft wide area, the distance between the arcs can be 10 ft. When water visibility is less than 3 ft, each diver may only be able to adequately search a 2- to 3- ft wide area so the distance between the arcs should only be 4–6 ft wide. Multiple diver/tender teams can be used concurrently to cover a large area. If this is the case, the arcs need to overlap between the teams to ensure a complete search of the area (fig. 19).

Advantages

Simple and easy to use.
Minimal amount of equipment needed.

Disadvantages

Submerged logs, large boulders, and other debris can tangle tender line.
Difficult to switch divers in the middle of the pattern.

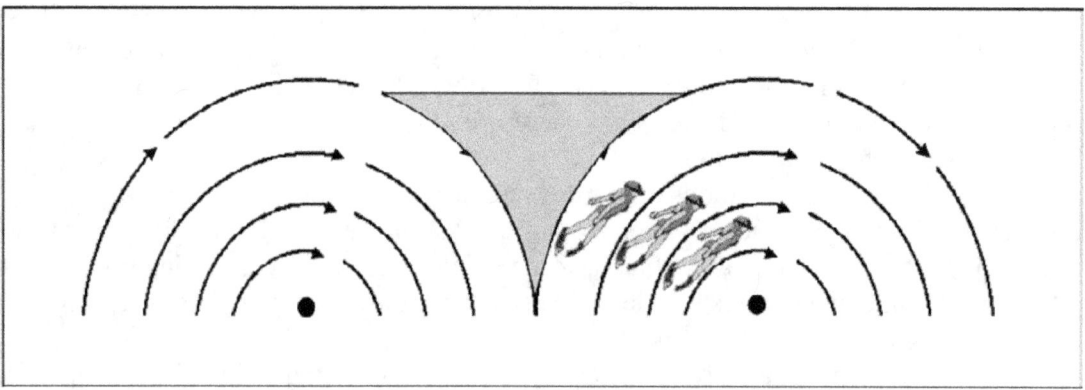

Figure 19. Drawing showing a standard arch sampling method. The area shown in gray represents the area that is not searched if the arcs are not overlapped.

Circle Search Method

The circle search method is similar to the arch search method and can be used to search open water sites like the area under floating docks. In this method, no tender is necessary. Instead, the divers control the distance between consecutive circles by letting out line that is connected to an anchor. Before beginning the first circle, the diver places a small, highly visible marker on the bottom. The diver knows when they have completed the first circle when the marker is re-located. The diver then picks up the marker, lets out more line, sets the marker down, and proceeds to search along the next circle in the pattern. This process is repeated until the entire area of interest is searched (fig. 20). Compass bearings can be used as an alternative to placing a marker on the bottom of the search area to determine when the circle is completed. To use this method, a compass bearing is taken at the beginning of the circle. When the same bearing is achieved at the end of the circle, the dive team moves to the next position to begin the next circle in the search pattern and a new compass bearing is taken. As was the case in the arc search method, the distance between circles is determined by the clarity of the water. It is best to have an anchor equipped with a mechanism that allows the line to move freely in a circle (fig. 21). If this is not part of the anchor design, the rope will get tangled around the anchor attachment point.

Advantages

Simple and easy to use.
Minimal amount of equipment needed, but anchor attachment point must move freely to prevent tangling.
No surface tender is needed to guide the diver.

Disadvantages

Submerged logs, large boulders, and other debris can tangle the line.
When multiple divers are used, this pattern must be overlapped to avoid missing areas.
Difficult to switch divers in the middle of the pattern.

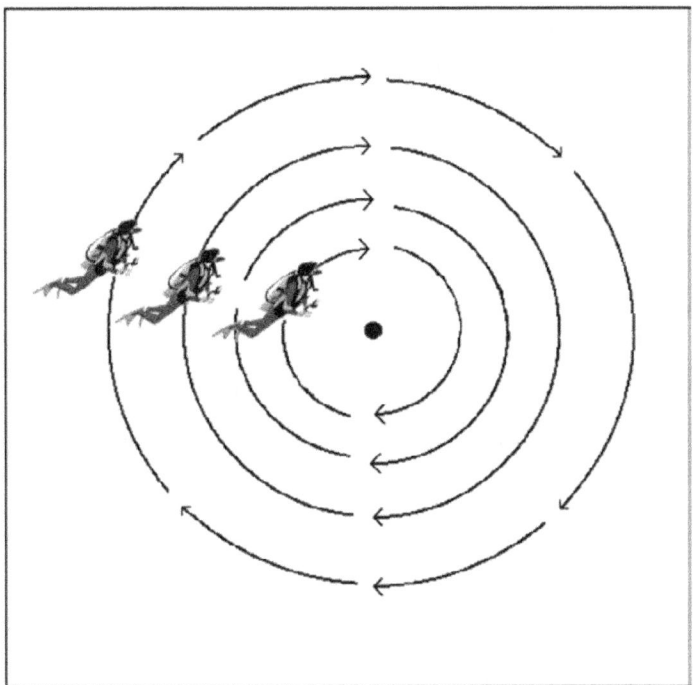

Figure 20. Drawing showing a standard circle search method.

Figure 21.   Photograph showing two pivot devices. One of these can be set on the bottom of a search area and used to guide the divers during the search when the circle or arc search methods are used. A rope is attached to the ring on the side of the pivot. The ring is welded to a sleeve that spins freely around the pivot, thereby preventing the rope from tangling during the search. A surface float and line can be attached to the ring at the top of the pivot and used as an accent/decent line. (Photograph courtesy of Carl Johansen, Assistant Team Leader, Sheriff's Diver Rescue and Recovery Team, Stevenson, Washington.)

Jackstay Search Method

This method is very effective for searching areas for small objects, like mussels. The word "jackstay" in nautical terms is used to describe a rail of wood or iron stretching along a yard of a vessel, to which the sails are fastened. When used to describe a search method, it is used to describe a rope stretched between two anchors. Figures 22 and 23 show the components that make up the jackstay system and how this system is commonly deployed. The system consists of two ascent/decent lines that connect surface buoys with the bottom anchors. The bottom anchors are connected to one another with a line, called the search line, which the divers use as a reference point during the search.

To conduct a search using this method, divers start at one anchor and search along the search line until they reach the second anchor. The second anchor is then move laterally along the substrate. The distance the anchor is moved depends on the clarity of the water and the size of the object divers are searched for. When searching for mussels, the anchor might be moved laterally one arms-length. Once this anchor is moved, the divers change direction and search back to the first anchor. The first anchor is then moved laterally one arms-length in the same direction the second anchor was moved and the divers search along the search line back to the second anchor. The anchors are moved laterally in this step-wise fashion until the area is completely searched. Figure 24 shows how moving the anchors in this manner creates a search pattern that overlaps itself several times. The overlapping search pattern makes this method very effective at finding small items. As effective as it is, many dive teams do not use it because it requires more equipment and time to set up and it can be confusing to implement unless divers have been trained in advance. However, the thoroughness of this search method may be worth the time it takes to train the divers and outfit them with the necessary equipment.

Advantages

Underwater debris does not interfere with the search. The search line can lie over the top of these obstacles.
Thorough search pattern in open water environment.
Surface buoy can be used by surface support staff to track the progress of the search.
Easy to switch divers in the middle of the search.

Disadvantages

More difficult to use and may require advanced training.
More equipment needed.
Time consuming.
This method results in the divers swimming through the same area multiple times. As a result, sediment can be stirred up by the divers and obscure the search area.

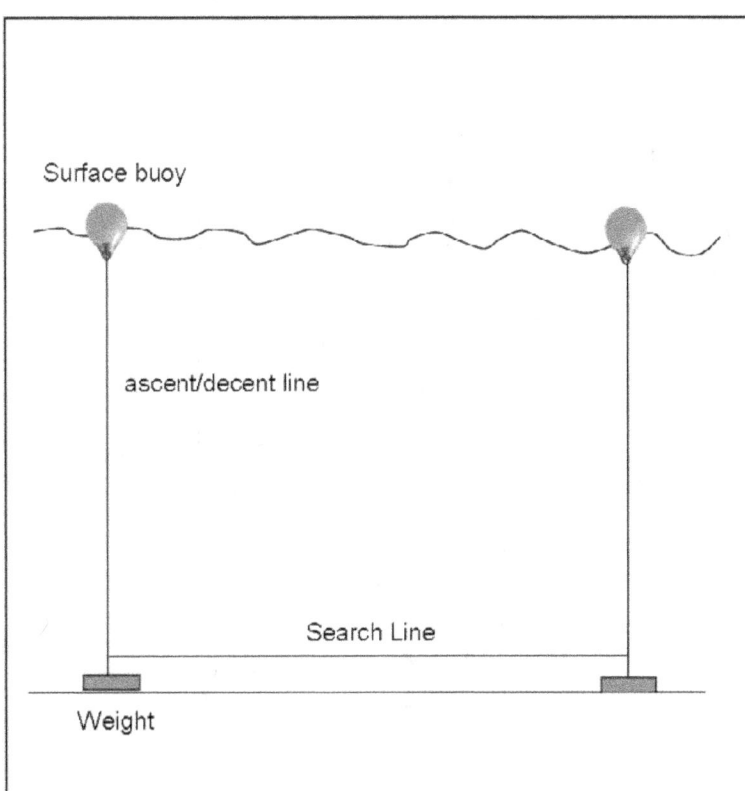

Figure 22. Drawing showing components of a jackstay search system.

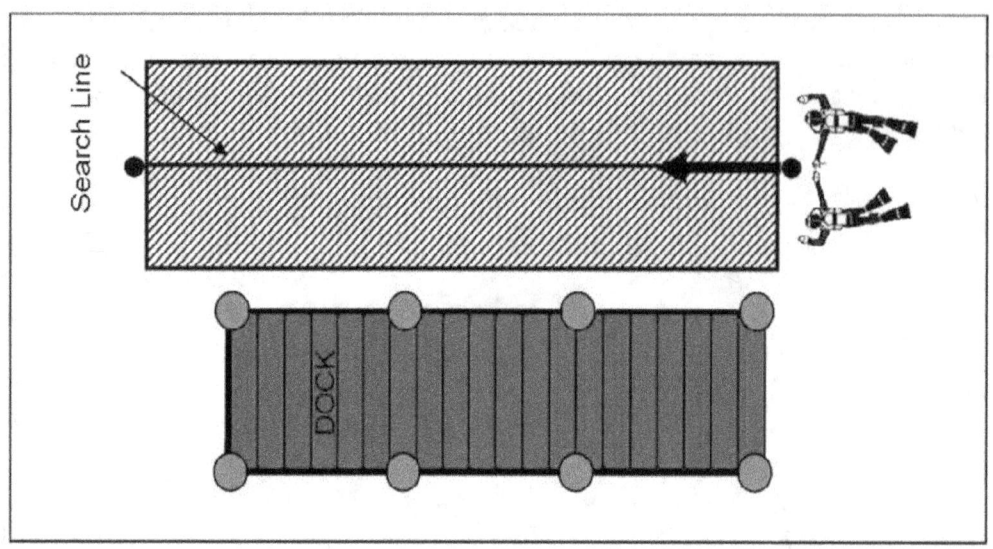

Figure 23. Drawing showing how a jackstay system can be used to search the area next to a dock.

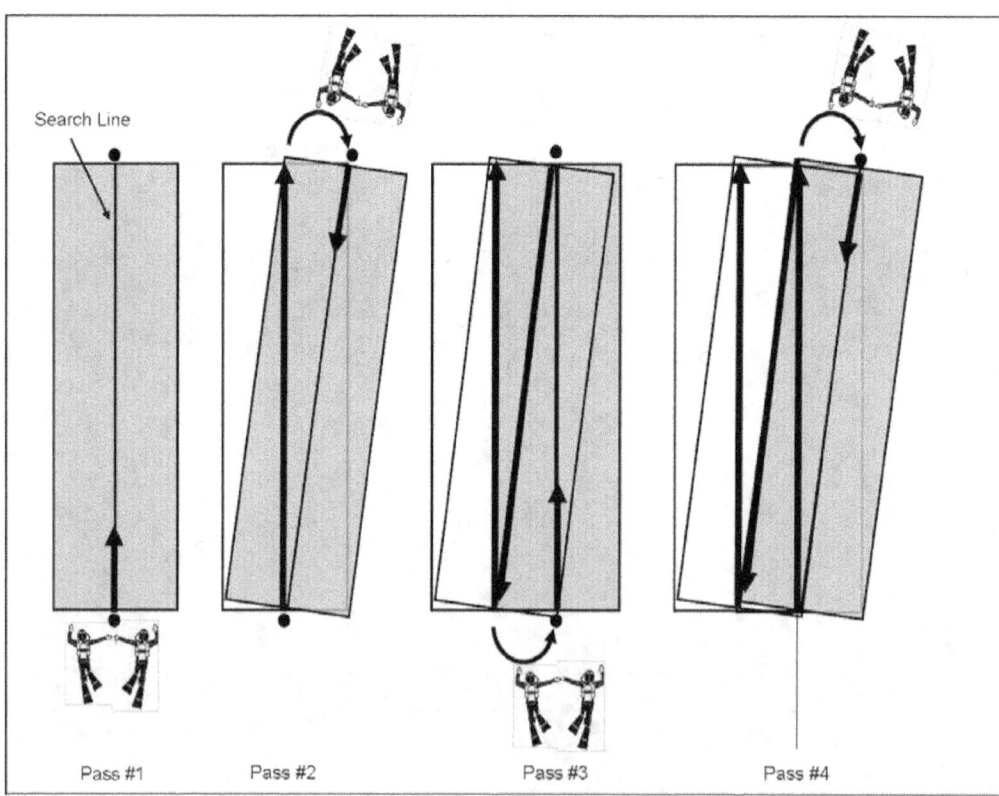

Figure 24. Drawing showing progression of moving a jackstay system during a search. The gray area represents the area that is being searched during each evolution of the pattern. Note the significant amount of overlap in the pattern using this system.

Dock Search Method

When searching docks for mussels, any water current should be used to the advantage of the diver to facilitate moving sediment away from the search area, not into areas that have not yet been searched. The series of images in figure 25 shows one approach to searching a dock. It is best to start at the deepest end of the dock and move to the shallow end because the divers will inevitably stir up sediment when they are searching the shallow area. To search large areas, multiple divers can be deployed simultaneously. In this case, individual teams should be briefed on the starting and stopping points to ensure areas are not excluded from the search.

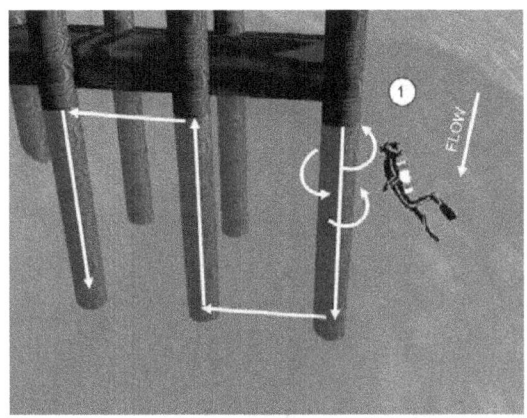
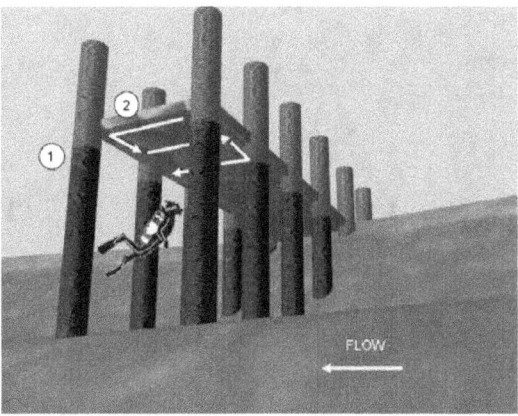
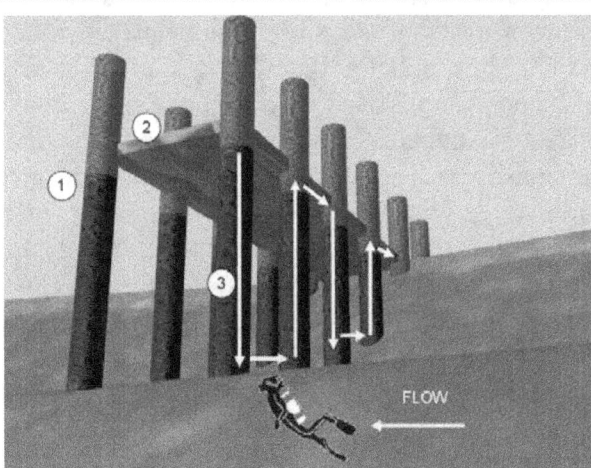

Figure 25.   Drawing showing one method for searching a dock for mussels. Note that the dock is searched in a manner that allows the flow of water to carry sediment displaced by the divers away from the search area.

Collecting Information about the Search Area

It is important to document information about the search environment. The requesting agency will need this information when reporting the results of the search and it can be useful for tracking the potential spread of invasive mussels. Below is a list of common information to collect during the search. Sample data sheets for recording this information are included in appendix 3.

Water temperature
Substrate characteristics
Air temperature
Weather conditions
Current
Visibility
Other species present during the search (i.e., fish, Asian clams, etc.)

Assessing the Probability of Detecting Mussels

Regardless of the search method used, it is helpful to have some measure of how successful the search was. A common way to estimate what the probability of detecting mussels was is to pre-seed the search area with items that are the same size, or smaller, than the item being searched for. When looking for mussels, one option is to seed the area with thumbtacks, which closely mimic a settled adult dreissenid mussel. The thumbtacks can be easily used to seed structures such as docks and can be placed under rocks or into submerged wood on the bottom. The number of thumbtacks used depends on the size of the search area. For example, a dock that is 50 ft long might be seeded with 10 thumbtacks on the dock and 5–10 thumbtacks on the surrounding substrate in the vicinity of the dock. Divers conducting the search should know that seed items have been deployed, but the number of items and their locations should not be revealed.

After the search is completed, the number of thumbtacks found and their locations can be used to estimate the probability of detecting mussels in the search area. For example, if 8 of the 10 thumbtacks on the dock were found, but only 2 of the 10 thumbtacks on the surrounding substrate were found, this would indicate that a relatively thorough search of the dock was accomplished (80 percent), but the surrounding area was not searched as well (20 percent). This information can be used to deploy additional divers in areas that were not adequately covered.

The thumbtacks should be numbered and their locations should be sketched on a site map (see appendix 3 for a data sheet that can be used to record the site map). This will allow any unfound thumbtacks to be recovered after the search and allow the divers to record the identification number of the thumbtack on their slate along with a brief description of where it was collected. Figure 26 shows the numbered thumbtacks and a container that can be used to collect them. The container should have a wide mouth to make it easy for the divers to open and close under water. The containers should be filled with water from the search area before the divers take them underwater. This will prevent the containers from floating towards the surface during the search. It is very important that the water used to fill the container is dumped back into the search area if the container was not used to collect samples. The empty container must be included in the equipment that is decontaminated after the dive. If the search area is infested with mussels, the water that is used to fill the containers can have microscopic veligers in it. If this water is transported to a different area, it can spread the infestation of mussels.

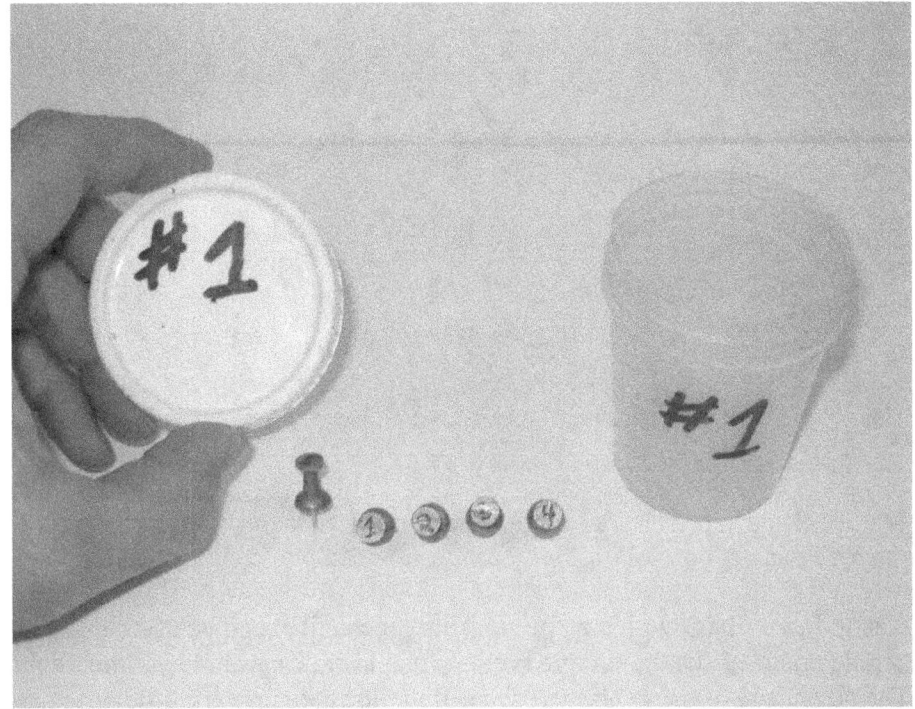

Figure 26.   Photograph of thumbtacks and container used to pre-seed the search area. Tacks can be used to estimate how efficient the search efforts were.

Seeding the site can provide useful information about how well the area was searched. However, it requires additional time and resources to implement and may not be feasible under all circumstances.

Collecting Mussel Samples

If divers find mussels, they should collect samples for verification. In anticipation of collecting samples, divers should be equipped with a mesh bag with several collection containers. Figure 27 shows a photograph of a small, wide-mouth container that is easy for divers to use. The containers need to be numbered before the dive. If a mussel is found, the diver can place it in one of the numbered containers and record information about where the sample was taken. Figure 27 shows an example of a slate that can be used to record the information. The slate has several writing surfaces in a compact design that is secured to the diver's wrist.

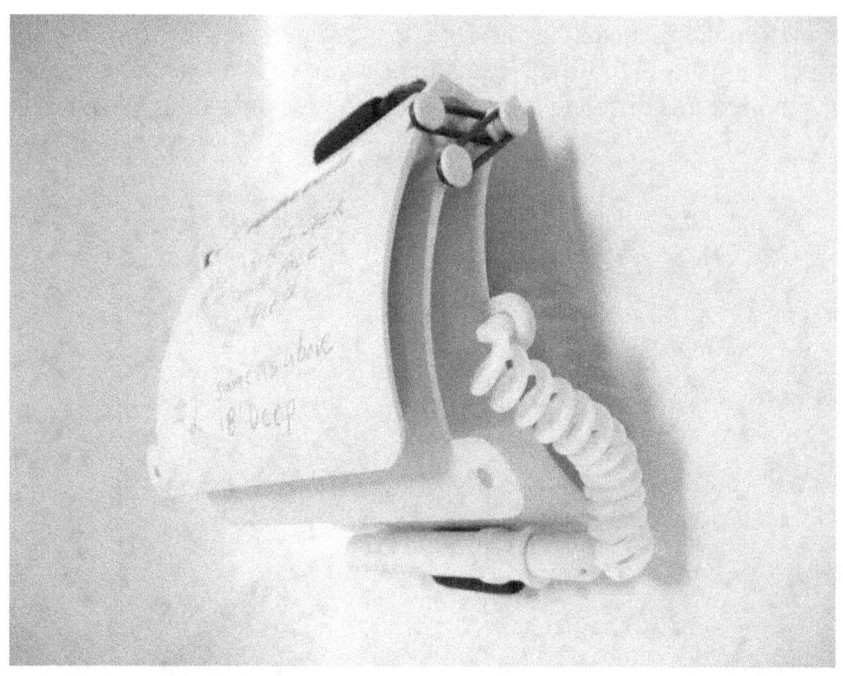

Figure 27. Photograph of a diver's slate. These can be used to record information during a search for mussels.

Plastic freezer bags with a zipper locking mechanism can be used instead of plastic sample bottles. Like the sample bottles, the plastic bags can be numbered prior to diving. The advantage of using plastic bags is that they take up very little space and are not buoyant so they do not need to be filled with water before diving. The disadvantage of using plastic bags is that some divers find it difficult to manipulate the zipper mechanism while wearing gloves. Furthermore, bags can burst when they are used to transport samples of water and mussels from the dive site to a laboratory.

Regardless of the type of sample container used, the diver needs to record minimum information about where the sample was collected. The diver should use an underwater slate to record a brief description of the location of where the sample was collected along with water depth and temperature. After the diver is out of the water, these notes are transferred to a label that is attached to the sample container (see appendix 3 for example of labels). After the container is labeled, the sample needs to be preserved for transportation to a laboratory for identification. To preserve the sample, the water is removed and replaced with a 70 percent isopropyl alcohol solution. Most of the over-the-counter alcohol that is available at drug stores is 70 percent isopropyl alcohol. When using alcohol to preserve samples, it is important to remember that it is flammable and the necessary precautions need to be implemented to prevent accidental fires. In addition, alcohol that is inadvertently spilled on the label will dissolve the ink if a standard pen is used. Permanent ink or pencil should be used to label all samples.

Another way to collect samples is to remove small rocks, sticks, or other substrate that the mussels are attached to. Figure 28 shows some examples of items that were removed during a survey in Lake Mead, Nevada. If this method is used, the items should be placed in a container with 70 percent isopropyl alcohol to preserve the mussels. If this is not possible, the sample can be allowed to air dry for an hour or two, and then heavily coated with a clear polyurethane or varnish. The items shown in figure 28 were coated with Minwax® water-based polyacrylic protective finish. The coating will prevent the mussels from falling off of the sample. If the mussels are allowed to sit out of the water for longer than an hour, they will die and fall off.

Figure 28. Photograph showing preserved samples of mussels. These items were removed during a mussel survey and then coated with Minwax® water-based polyacrylic protective finish.

When samples are taken in the open water environment, it is best to place a marker buoy at the sample location to provide a reference point. There are many suitable surface marker buoys available and the one that works best is the one that the divers are most familiar with. Figure 29 shows some examples of marker buoys.

Figure 29. Examples of marker buoys that can be used to identify where samples were collected.

Depending on the level of infestation, it might be necessary to count the number of mussels seen by each diver. If this is the case, one simple way to accomplish this is to outfit the divers with tally counters. Several models exist that are inexpensive, made of plastic, and can be used underwater (fig. 30). The divers should be instructed to collect several mussel samples for verification and count all mussels seen during the survey using the tally counter. The need to count the number of mussels seen by the diver will be determined by the agency overseeing the search. If the objective of the search is to simply verify that mussels are present in the area, it is not necessary to count them. However, divers may be asked to count the number of mussels seen during the search so the agency overseeing the mission can have a general idea of the number of mussels in the area.

Figure 30.   Example of a tally counter. Divers can use these to record the number of mussels seen during a search.

In addition to counting mussels and obtaining a few adult mussels for verification, documenting other observations about the mussel population can be very useful to managers trying to develop a strategy to contain the infestation. Divers should note the variation in the size of the mussels, if the mussels appear in clumps or as solitary individuals, the presence of mussels that appear dead, and the presence of empty mussel shells in the search area. One way to determine if a mussel is dead is to touch the mussel while the shell is open. If the mussel does not close its shells after being touched, it is likely dead.

Underwater photography can be a useful way to document the presence of mussels and gather useful information about the characteristics of the population (fig. 31). However, underwater photography should not be the only way to verify the presence of mussels and samples should still be collected during the initial search. Although capturing quality photographs of underwater specimens can be difficult, technological advances in video equipment has made it easier. Most cameras are capable of capturing images in relatively low visibility conditions. If divers use underwater photography equipment, they should place a ruler or other common object in the field of view to serve as a reference and reflect the scale of the objects that are being photographed.

Figure 31. Example of underwater video equipment. Photograph can be used to document the presence of mussels during a search.

Regardless of the sampling method, divers need to know that transferring invasive species without a permit is a crime in many States and can result in penalties and fines. Divers need to work with their State and Federal agencies to obtain authorization to keep a mussel as a souvenir.

Decontamination of Equipment

It is very important to decontaminate all equipment that was used during a search for mussels. Although adult mussels are relatively easy to see on dive equipment, the larval stage (called veligers) is only visible using a microscope. The larva can live anywhere water can pool. The inside of the diver's buoyancy compensator (BC) is a good example (fig. 32). Appendix 4 outlines the methods used by USGS divers to decontaminate equipment. Another source of information for decontamination of equipment and boats can be found at the California Department of Fish and Game website (*www.dfg.ca.gov/invasives/quaggamussel*). Decontamination of equipment should be overseen by someone familiar with the process.

Figure 32. Photograph of a typical SCUBA Buoyancy Control (BC) vest. Extra diligence needs to be applied to properly decontaminate the internal bladder of the BC to prevent the spread of mussels.

Acknowledgments

The author would like to thank the following people for their assistance during the preparation of this document and their review and comments on early drafts: Bryan Moore, National Park Service, Lake Mead, Nevada; Marc Blouin, USGS, National Dive Safety Program Manager; Arne Gonser, Sergeant, Skamania County Sheriff's Office; Scott Smith, USGS Ecology Section Chief; Paul Heimowitz, USFWS Aquatic Invasive Species and Research Coordinator; Dennis Otsuka, Metropolitan Water District of Southern California; Dan Marelli, Scientific Diving International; Dave Lamb, Lake Ecologist, Coeur d'Alene Tribe. The author also is grateful to Matthew Sholtis, Lynn Casal, Nick Swyers, Rachel Reagan, Dena Gadomski, and Dennis Rondorf at the Columbia River Research Laboratory for their assistance in providing material for this document and editorial review.

References Cited

Benson, A.J., Richerson, M.M., and Maynard, E., 2010, Dreissena rostriformis bugensis. U.S. Geological Survey database, accessed November 9, 2010, at http://nas.er.usgs.gov/queries/FactSheet.aspx?speciesID=95.

California Department of Fish and Game, no date, Invasive Speices Program: California Department of Fish and Game database, accessed October 18, 2010, at http://www.dfg.ca.gov/invasives/quaggamussel/

Henke, S.E., 1998, The effect of multiple search items and item abundance on efficiency of human searches: Journal of Herpetology, v. 32, p. 112-115.

Nedeau, E.J., Smith, A.K., Stone, Jen, and Jepsen, Sarina, 2009, Freshwater mussels of the Pacific Northwest, Second Edition: The Xerces Society for Invertebrate Conservation, 52 p., accessed October 15, 2010, at http://www.xerces.org/wp-content/uploads/2009/06/pnw_mussel_guide_2nd_edition.pdf.

U.S. Geological Survey, 2009, Nonindiginous Aquatic Species Program (NAS): U.S. Geological Survey database, accessed October 18, 2010, at http://nas.er.usgs.gov/taxgroup/mollusks/zebramussel/.

Appendix 1 – Example of USGS Diving Reciprocity Form.

REQUEST FOR DIVING RECIPROCITY FORM
VERIFICATION OF DIVER TRAINING AND EXPERIENCE

A scientific diver, who is currently authorized to dive for the USGS and meets the requirements for scientific diving of another host organization, may apply to the USGS Diving Safety Board (DSB) or the Diving Safety Officer (DSO) to be considered for diving reciprocity as a visiting diver. Upon review of the diver's credentials, records, and justification, the DSB/DSO may grant approval for diving reciprocity with the host organization. The visiting bureau diver will meet or exceed all requirements and comply with the diving regulations of the host organization's Diving Safety Manual unless previously arranged by both of the organization's Diving Safety (Control) Boards.

The host organization has the right to approve or deny this request and may require, at a minimum, a checkout dive with the Diving Safety Officer (DSO) or designee of the host organization. If the request is denied, the host organization should notify the DSO of the visiting diver the reason for the denial. The DSO for the visiting scientific diver has confirmed the following information:

(Date – mm/dd/yyyy)

_____ Written scientific diving examination

_____ Last diving medical examination. Expiration date: _____

_____ Most recent checkout dive

_____ SCUBA regulator/equipment service/test

_____ CPR training (Agency): _____. Expiration date: _____

_____ Oxygen administration (Agency): _____. Expiration date: _____

_____ First aid for diving (Agency): _____. Expiration date: _____

_____ Date of last Dive

Number of dives completed within previous 12 months? __

Depth certification: ____

Are there any restrictions? __ Yes __ No
    If yes, explain:

Please check any pertinent specialty certifications:

__Dry suit	__Divemaster	__Altitude
__Nitrox	__Instructor	__Ice/Polar
__Mixed gas	__EMT	__Cave
__Closed circuit	__Dive Accident Management	__Night
__Saturation	__Chamber operator	__Other (Specify)
__Decompression	__Lifesaving	

Name of Diver: _____ Emergency Information: (To notify in an emergency)

Name: _____ Relationship: _____

Telephone: (work) _____ (home) _____

Address: _____

This is to verify that the above individual, _____ (insert diver's name) is currently authorized to dive for the U.S. Geological Survey and meets the requirements set fort for diving with the host organization: _____.

Diving Safety Officer: _____ _____
          (Signature)   (Date)

        _____ _____
           (Print)   (Telephone)

        _____ _____
           (FAX)   (E-mail)

Appendix 2 – Sample Check Lists

The following sheets are included in this document as examples that can be used during searches for mussels.

PRE-DIVE EQUIPMENT
CHECKLIST

Date _____ Time _____
Location_____
Name and contact information of
  person overseeing dive operations _____

What each diver should bring:

- O Buoyancy Compensator (BC)
- O Regulators
- O Weight Belt/Integrated Weights
- O Dive Harness
- O Mask
- O Fins
- O Snorkel
- O Exposure Suit (Wet or Dry Suit)
- O Tanks
- O Hood and Gloves
- O Flashlights (at least two)
- O Extra Batteries for Flashlights
- O Mesh Collection Bag
- O Cutting Devices (Scissors and Knife)
- O Underwater Writing Slate
- O Food and Water
- O Life Jacket

Additional equipment that the dive coordinator/dive master needs to bring:

O Diver emergency oxygen kit, first aid kit, and backboard.

O Dive flags

O Means of communication (that is, radio, cellular telephone, satellite telephone)

O Camera

O Data sheets

O Sample containers and 70 percent isopropyl alcohol for preserving samples

O Items to pre-seed the search area

O Equipment for conducting search patterns

      O Ropes

      O Floats

      O Anchors

O Decontamination equipment

O Lockout/tag out supplies (see appendix 5)

O If boats will be used in the search, the Dive Operations Coordinator needs to ensure that the boat operators are aware of the special consideration when divers are in the water, ensure proper communications between the dive teams and boat operators, and ensure the boats are properly decontaminated after the search is complete.

PRE-DIVE CHECKLIST

Date _____ Time _____
Location_____
Name and contact information of
  person conducting pre-dive check _____

O   Define dive mission, objectives, and goals

O   Ensure that all divers are qualified by having the proper training and experience to safely
     complete the required tasks

O   Explain dive site boundaries

O   Review dive conditions: Wind, currents, waves, and visibility
     o   Specific hazards of the dive site: Marine life (animals and plants), caves, currents,
         wrecks, other vessels.
     o   Evaluate and discuss potential for entrapment, entanglement, or other physical or
         mechanical hazards
     o   Evaluate and discuss potential for bottom obstructions or dangerous bottom conditions
     o   Evaluate and discuss potential for strong currents, low visibility, thermoclines, and
         surges
     o   Evaluate and discuss potential for contamination or exposure to pollution (such as,
         petroleum products or biological and chemical hazards)

O   Review procedures for water entry and exit, and location of descent/ascent and float lines

O   Dive buddies paired up and review "Buddy Check"
     o   Buoyancy – BC is functional and partially inflated for entry
     o   Weights – Weight type (integrated or belt) and release is free for access
     o   Releases – All clips, Velcro, buckles, and tank straps are secured
     o   Air – Air is on and flow is tested. Note volume of air in tank
     o   Final assessment. Is your buddy physically and mentally ready for the tasks?
     o   Do you know your buddy's gear? Backup regulator, weight release method, and cutting
         devices

O   Maximum depth and bottom time, minimal "return to surface" tanks pressure

O   Procedures if separated from dive group or surfaced and caught in a current

O   Review hand signals

O   Diver emergency and recall procedures

O   Oxygen kit, first aid kit, and backboard on site

O   Ensure appropriate dive flags are prominently displayed

O   Means of communication (radio, cellular telephone, landline telephone, Satellite phone)

POST-DIVE CHECKLIST

Date _____ Time _____
Location_____
Name and contact information of
 person conducting post-dive check _____

- O   All divers safely out of water
- O   Dive team buddies stay together for a minimum of 1 hour to monitor post-dive condition
- O   Strike dive flags
- O   Recover and stow all support equipment
- O   Transfer samples to agency representative
- O   Ensure that all dive equipment is thoroughly cleaned and properly stowed.
- O   Conduct a dive debrief with all divers
    - o Identify problems experienced during the dive
    - o Lessons learned for future missions
    - o Data and specimens documented and turned over to appropriate person
- O   Monitor divers for signs and symptoms of pressure-related illnesses or injuries
- O   Remind divers to seek medical attention if they experience dive related injury symptoms after leaving the dive site

Appendix 3 – Sample Data Sheets

The following information contains examples of data sheets that can aid in documenting searches for mussels.

Site Map Data sheet

Date_____   Time_____   Dive #_____

Your Name_____   Location_____

Sketch of Search area

Note _____
_____
_____
_____
_____
_____
_____
_____
_____
_____

Documenting Environmental Data of Dive Site

Location_____

Date_____   **Time**_____

Collected by (name and contact information)
_____
_____
_____

Water temperature (specify $^{\circ}$C or $^{\circ}$F) _____

Substrate characteristics
(bedrock – hard) (bedrock – shale) (boulder - immovable, generally over 1 meter in diameter)
(cobble - movable), (silt/mud)
_____
_____
_____
_____

Air temperature _____

Weather conditions
_____
_____
_____

Current
_____
_____
_____

Visibility
_____
_____
_____

Other notes (species present fish etc).
_____
_____
_____
_____
_____
_____

Label for sample containers

Mussel Sample

Location:_____

Date:_____ Collected By:_____

Depth Range:_____

Substrate:_____

Water Temperature:_____

Preservative:_____

Comments:_____

Mussel Sample

Location:_____

Date:_____ Collected By:_____

Depth Range:_____

Substrate:_____

Water Temperature:_____

Preservative:_____

Comments:_____

Mussel Sample

Location:_____

Date:_____ Collected By:_____

Depth Range:_____

Substrate:_____

Water Temperature:_____

Preservative:_____

Comments:_____

Mussel Sample

Location:_____

Date:_____ Collected By:_____

Depth Range:_____

Substrate:_____

Water Temperature:_____

Preservative:_____

Comments:_____

Mussel Sample

Location:_____

Date:_____ Collected By:_____

Depth Range:_____

Substrate:_____

Water Temperature:_____

Preservative:_____

Comments:_____

Mussel Sample

Location:_____

Date:_____ Collected By:_____

Depth Range:_____

Substrate:_____

Water Temperature:_____

Preservative:_____

Comments:_____

Mussel Sample

Location:_____

Date:_____ Collected By:_____

Depth Range:_____

Substrate:_____

Water Temperature:_____

Preservative:_____

Comments:_____

Mussel Sample

Location:_____

Date:_____ Collected By:_____

Depth Range:_____

Substrate:_____

Water Temperature:_____

Preservative:_____

Comments:_____

Appendix 4 – USGS Decontamination Procedure.

STANDARD OPERATING PROCEDURES

U. S. Geological Survey
Great Lakes Science Center
1451 Green Road, Ann Arbor, MI 48105

Revised September 19, 2002

A procedure for the decontamination of SCUBA diving equipment and underwater gear after diving in waters containing zebra mussels (*Dreissena polymorpha*) and other exotic species of Dreissenid.

This Standard Operating Procedure (SOP) is intended to provide a step-by-step procedure for the decontamination of SCUBA diving equipment after its use in waters infested with zebra mussels. Current information regarding geographic areas of zebra mussel infestations is available from the U.S. Geological Survey (2009) Non-indigenous Aquatic Species (NAS) website (http://nas.er.usgs.gov/taxgroup/mollusks/zebramussel/).

Overview:

In order to avoid the spread of zebra mussels to non-infested waters via SCUBA diving equipment and underwater sampling gear, a protocol must be designed and implemented.

Responsibility:

All USGS procedures for the decontamination of SCUBA equipment will strictly adhere to and follow all USGS requirements. All USGS authorized divers will be responsible their dive gear and underwater equipment.

Dive Gear and Equipment:
Wetsuits and Drysuits
Buoyancy Compensators
Tanks (including boots and protective mesh)
Regulators and gauges
Mask, Fins, Snorkel
Cameras and video equipment
Sampling devices

Procedures:

(1) All dive gear and equipment used in zebra mussel infested waters should be inspected for the presence of adult zebra mussels. If found, adult zebra mussels should be removed, dried (or killed using another effective method) and disposed of in a manner that prevents introduction into local waters. All dive gear must be washed thoroughly by soaking in warm, soapy water and rinsing in warm, chlorinated tap water. Water temperatures greater than 110 °F have been found to be effective for killing larval zebra mussels, however, water temperatures greater than 120°F should not be used as it may damage certain temperature–sensitive dive gear and void some manufacturer's warranties. Acidic or basic solutions (including vinegar or bleach) also should not be used as they may compromise the integrity of thermoplastic materials. Buoyancy compensators must be flushed internally with warm tap water and dried completely using standard procedures as recommended by the manufacturer. Commercial dive gear cleaners, such as wetsuit shampoos, may be used in the decontamination process. Drains in washing facilities must be attached to a source for wastewater treatment (municipal sewer) and must not discharge into external waters.

(2) All dive gear and equipment must be completely dry for at least 24 hours before use in waters where there is no zebra mussel infestation. Note: wetsuit seams should be closely inspected to insure that the material is completely dry.

Contact information:

Marc A. Blouin
Fishery Research Biologist / Diving Safety Officer
mblouin@usgs.gov
U.S. Geological Survey
Great Lakes Science Center
1451 Green Road, Ann Arbor, MI 48105
734-994-8780 fax
734-214-7248 work

Appendix 5 – Lock-Out/Tag-Out Procedures

This is a brief overview of basic lock-out/tag-out procedure. The purpose of this overview is to familiarize the members of the search team with the basic steps for preventing the accidental operation of equipment that could injure SCUBA divers during an underwater search.

When SCUBA diving near dams, power plants, pumping plants, or diversion structures with mechanical or electrical features that could pose a hazard to divers, a technical representative responsible for the operation of the equipment must be present or in direct communication to assist the divers.

During the pre-dive briefing, the dive operations coordinator will inform all divers about the potential hazards and the procedures that will be implemented to prevent the accidental operation of equipment in the dive area.

The technical representative will identify the electrical and/or physical control points for energizing the feature that is to be tagged out. For example, this could be an electrical breaker for controlling a pump that draws water through an intake pipe and/or a valve that controls the flow of water through a pipe or other water conveyance structure.

A physical lock and appropriate warning tag will be fastened to the control point. Basic lock-out/tag-out kits are available from numerous vendors that are specifically designed for this purpose (fig. 3-1). After the lock and tag have been secured, both the technical representative and the dive operations coordinator will sign the tag indicating that the proper procedures have been conducted and it is safe for divers to enter the area.

After dive operations are complete, the technical representative and the dive operations coordinator must mutually agree that it is safe to remove the lock and tag, thereby releasing the control point for normal operations. The dive operations coordinator and the technical representative must both be present to remove the lock and tag. No other person or persons have the authority to release the control point for normal operations.

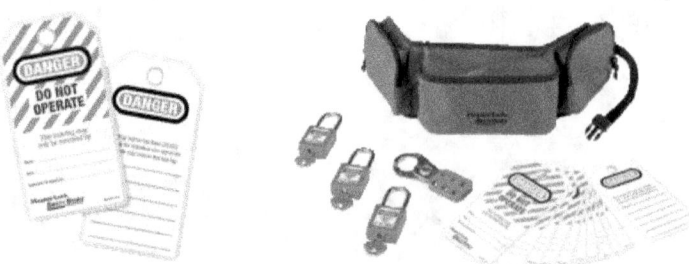

Figure 3-1. Examples of tags (left) and lock-out/tag-out kits (right) that are used to prevent the operation of hazardous equipment while divers are in the water.